Daily Devotions

Kele Pandolfe

1

Dedication

To: Colton & Kylee may you be rooted in who He is, expectant of His promises. Rising as you see your value and worth through the truth of His Word.

To all those standing on the threshold. Rising, expectant and ready to be firmly planted.

Table of Contents

Introduction

Hello friend. The fact that you have picked up this book already gives my heart a gravitational pull towards yours. Proverbs 2:1-6 reads:

"If you receive my words and treasure up my commands within you, making your ear attentive to wisdom and inclining your heart to understanding, yes if you call out for insight and raise your voice for understanding, if you seek it like silver and search for it as hidden treasure, then you will understand the fear of the Lord, and find the knowledge of God. For the Lord gives wisdom, from His mouth come knowledge and understanding."

This right here, is it! "Receive, treasure up, attentive, call out for, raise your voice, and seek it." Each of these words & phrases should excite us, give us strength. We are told clearly that when we seek it like silver, we will have proper fear, wisdom, knowledge and understanding.

This question has been asked of me many, many times "How are you not broken, sad, lost etc., when there has been so much heartache & loss in your life?" It is one thing to say, "Well prayer, relationship and a daily devotion of course." Then the next question would be, "What does that look like for you?"

After many encounters like this, God kept whispering a phrase, on repeat, "Show them". As I so eloquently argued back, "There are many resources out there. Why would I add to it?" You see where this was headed. God wins... He always does, and I am so undeserving of His patience with my questioning heart and mercy over my abilities. As you hold this devotional, know it comes from a place of oneness. My desire is to humbly pass along to you what God has graciously taken me from and continues to walk me towards. HIS WORD.

Without it, I would be a puddle on the floor, filled with self-loathing filth. Within it, I am a seeker of what is bigger and broader than me. We are each walking "life". What that looks like for you bears a differing weight than what it looks like for me. Each of us different in many ways, yet remarkably more similar than we care to admit.

We were created to worship, to create, commune. When we have that focus out of alignment, we suffer. Our suffering seeps into self-satisfaction, then we are satiated with self. My prayer is that this little guide will deepen your understanding of who God is, what He continues to fulfill through His promises and how He Speaks those truths over each of us to walk in His knowledge boldly and unashamed.

This devotional is split into 3 parts to walk you along this journey. Part 1: Rooted in God, Part 2: Rooted in His Promises, Part 3: Rooted in His Truth. When we seek to be conformed into the image of Christ it takes receiving His word with an attentive ear and an inclined heart. Loving His word above all else. Knowing His character, which reforms our character, and makes us obedient vessels, hungry, seeking to love as He loved.

This devotional is the answer to those questions friend. A daily empting out of me and a filling up of Him & lathering in His Word. Because the hard days WILL come. People WILL hurt us. Questions will go unanswered. Yet, when we are seeking the knowledge of who HE is, what HE promises and what IS truth, the broken days have a balm waiting and ready for healing to begin.

In His Grace, Kele

Part 1

Rooted in God

W e as finite people see, from a very limited & tainted lens. Our identity is often what was spoken over or to us in our lifetime. Words become rooted and a part of how we see ourselves from the inside out. They can form us into "who" we see ourselves to be, our identity.

Along our journeys, be in 6 decades or two, we experienced a multitude of encounters with words from others, from our inner critic, looks, gestures, and decisions that have shaped what we call "us".

In part 1 of this devotional, we are going to take a deep dive into Who God is... Why, because in order to know who we are, we have to know who He is. Because we are His and we are made in His image. Born to serve, enjoy and glorify all our days. That can't be done to its fullest capacity... if we lack knowledge of His character, who He is.

We will take a giant leap back and stand at the threshold to a new mindset, a new space. To know you CAN replace false identities you have embraced to this point, replacing false narratives with Gods truth and identity.

As we move day by day through WHO God is, we will be focusing upon scripture that highlights His character. Take your time, read through each day at your pace. There is no timeline here. This is why you will see no dates, I don't believe God meant for His word to have a shelf life. Set a pace that lets the Spirit breathe into it.

Scripture is alive and breathing and wants to expand your soul with its beauty and knowledge. Give it time to do just that. Let it breathe into your space, season, and your day. Let's get to know then absorb the one who holds it all in the palm of His hand.

This section is set up for you to fully engage in scripture, to hear HIS voice. I have purposefully not used my words or opinions through this section, as the purpose is of being "rooted" in the Word. To READ the word. Each day will have a scripture, then space for you to reflect in these ways.

> *Read:* Asking the Holy Spirit to open your heart to the truth of the word. I read my daily passage a couple of times, quietly and then out loud.
> *Write:* Use the space provided to write out the passage.
> *Reflect:* What does this passage say about God? His character - who he is.
> *Engage:* Spend quiet minutes just hearing His voice wash over you, speaking into your heart and mind. It may be a word from the passage or more. Just listen.

Lord,

Enlighten what is dark

Strengthen what is weak

Mend what is broken

Bind what is bruised

Heal what is sick

Revive peace within me

Amen

Healer

Jehovah Rapha

Day 1

Healer

Matthew 5:4

Blessed are those who mourn, for they shall be comforted.

Write it:

Reflect:

Engage:

Day 2

Healer

Psalm 147:3

e heals the brokenhearted and binds up their wounds.

Write it:

Reflect:

Engage:

Psalm 73:26

y flesh and my heart may fail, but God is the strength of my heart, and my portion forever.

Write it:

Reflect:

Engage:

Day 4

Healer

Psalm 107:28

T hen they cried out to the Lord in their trouble; and He brought them out of their distress.

Write it:

Reflect:

Engage

Day 5

Healer

Psalm 86:3-4

Be gracious to me, O Lord, for to you do I cry all the day. ⁴ Gladden the soul of your servant, for to you, O Lord, do I lift up my soul.

Write it:

Reflect:

Engage:

Restorer

Jehovah Mekoddishkem

Day 1

Restorer

1 Peter 5:10

A nd the God of all grace, who called you to His eternal glory, in Christ, after you have suffered a little while, will humble himself, restore you and make you strong, firm and steadfast.

Write it:

Reflect:

Engage:

Day 2

Restorer

Psalm 147:3

He heals the brokenhearted and binds up their wounds.

Write it:

Reflect:

Engage:

Joel 2:25-26

I will restore[d] to you the years that the swarming locust has eaten, the hopper, the destroyer, and the cutter, my great army, which I sent among you. "You shall eat in plenty and be satisfied, and praise the name of the LORD your God, who has dealt wondrously with you.
And my people shall never again be put to shame.

Write it:

Reflect:

Engage:

Day 4

Restorer

Psalm 23:3

 He restores my soul, He leads me in the paths of righteousness for His name sake.

Write it:

Reflect:

Engage:

Day 5

Psalm 51:12

 estore to me the joy of your salvation and uphold me a willing spirit.

Write it:

Reflect:

Engage:

He who Sees

El Roi

Day 1

Psalm 146:9

T he LORD *watches over the alien and sustains the fatherless,*
and the widow. But He frustrates the ways of the wicked.

Write it:

Reflect:

Engage:

Day 2

He who Sees

Psalm 23:1-3

T he LORD is my shepherd; I shall not want. [2]He makes me lie down in green pastures. He leads me beside still waters.[a] [3] He restores my soul. He leads me in paths of righteousness[b] for his name's sake.

Write it:

Reflect:

Engage:

Day 3

He who Sees

Psalm 10:14

But you do see, for you note mischief and vexation, that you may take it into your hands;
to you the helpless commits himself; you have been the helper of the fatherless.

Write it:

Reflect:

Engage:

Day 4

He who Sees

Proverbs 15:3

The eyes of the LORD are in every place,
keeping watch on the evil and the good.

Write it:

Reflect:

Engage:

Psalm 32:8

I will instruct you and teach you in the way you should go; I will counsel you with my eye upon you.

Write it:

Reflect:

Engage:

Merciful

Jehovah Shammah

Merciful

Isaiah 54: 10

F or the mountains may depart and the hills be removed, but my steadfast love shall not depart from you, and my covenant of peace shall not be removed," says the LORD, who has compassion on you.

Write it:

Reflect:

Engage:

Day 2

Merciful

Psalm 119:7-8

I will praise you with an upright heart, when I learn your righteous rules.[b] 8 I will keep your statutes; do not utterly forsake me!

Write it:

Reflect:

Engage:

Day 3

Psalm 6:9-10

T he LORD has heard my cry for mercy; the LORD accepts my prayer. All my enemies will be ashamed and dismayed, they will turn back in sudden disgrace.

Write it:

Reflect:

Engage:

Day 4

Merciful

Psalm 31:7-8

I will rejoice and be glad in your steadfast love, because you have seen my affliction; you have known the distress of my soul, [8] and you have not delivered me into the hand of the enemy; you have set my feet in a broad place.

Write it:

Reflect:

Engage:

1 Timothy 1:16

But I received mercy for this reason, that in me, as the foremost, Jesus Christ might display his perfect patience as an example to those who were to believe in him for eternal life.

Write it:

Reflect:

Engage:

Strength

El Sali

Psalm 119:28

y soul melts away for sorrow; strengthen me according to your word!

Write it:

Reflect:

Engage:

Day 2

Strength

Psalm 28:7-8

The LORD is my strength and my shield; in him my heart trusts, and I am helped; my heart exults, and with my song I give thanks to him. The LORD is the strength of his people;[b] he is the saving refuge of his anointed.

Write it:

Reflect:

Engage:

39

Day 3

Strength

Psalm 18:1-2

I love you, O LORD, my strength. [2] The LORD is my rock and my fortress and my deliverer, my God, my rock, in whom I take refuge, my shield, and the horn of my salvation, my stronghold.

Write it:

Reflect:

Engage:

Day 4

Strength

Psalm 29:11

ay the LORD give strength to his people! May the LORD bless[d] his people with peace!

Write it:

Reflect:

Engage:

Day 5

Psalm 68:35

A wesome is God from his[h] sanctuary; the God of Israel—he is the one who gives power and strength to his people. Blessed be God!

Write it:

Reflect:

Engage:

Protector

Jehovah Nissi

Day 1

Protector

Isaiah 41:10

Fear not, for I am with you; be not dismayed, for I am your God; I will strengthen you, I will help you, I will uphold you with my righteous right hand.

Write it:

Reflect:

Engage:

Day 2

Protector

Psalm 5:11-12

But let all who take refuge in you rejoice; let them ever sing for joy, and spread your protection over them, that those who love your name may exult in you. [12] For you bless the righteous, O LORD; you cover him with favor as with a shield.

Write it:

Reflect:

Engage:

Day 3

Psalm 57:1

Be merciful to me, O God, be merciful to me, for in you my soul takes refuge; in the shadow of your wings I will take refuge, till the storms of destruction pass by.

Write it:

Reflect:

Engage:

Day 4

Psalm 128:4

 ehold, thus shall the man be blessed who fears the LORD.

Write it:

Reflect:

Engage:

Day 5

Protector

2 Corinthians 4:8-9

We are afflicted in every way, but not crushed; perplexed, but not driven to despair; [9] persecuted, but not forsaken; struck down, but not destroyed.

Write it:

Reflect:

Engage:

Pursuer

Jehovah Raah

Psalm 119:89-90

Forever, O LORD, your word is firmly fixed in the heavens. ⁹⁰ Your faithfulness endures to all generations; you have established the earth, and it stands fast.

Write it:

Reflect:

Engage:

Day 2

Pursuer

Nahum 1:7

The LORD is good, a stronghold in the day of trouble; he knows those who take refuge in him.

Write it:

Reflect:

Engage:

Day 3

Psalm 94:12-13

Blessed is the man whom you discipline, O LORD, and whom you teach out of your law, [13] to give him rest from days of trouble, until a pit is dug for the wicked.

Write it:

Reflect:

Engage:

Day 4

Pursuer

Romans 8:27

And he who searches hearts knows what is the mind of the Spirit, because[a] the Spirit intercedes for the saints according to the will of God.

Write it:

Reflect:

Engage:

Day 5

Pursuer

Romans 8:14

F or all who are led by the Spirit of God are sons[i] of God.

Write it:

Reflect:

Engage:

Jehovah Shammah

Hope

Psalm 130:5-7

I wait for the LORD, my soul waits, and in his word I hope; ⁶ my soul waits for the Lord
more than watchmen for the morning, more than watchmen for the morning. ⁷ O Israel, hope in the LORD! For with the LORD there is steadfast love,
and with him is plentiful redemption.

Write it:

Reflect:

Engage:

Day 2

Hope

Psalm 16:9

Therefore my heart is glad, and my whole being[s] rejoices; my flesh also dwells secure.

Write it:

Reflect:

Engage:

Day 3

Hope

Psalm 42:11

Why are you cast down, O my soul, and why are you in turmoil within me? Hope in God; for I shall again praise him, my salvation and my God.

Write it:

Reflect:

Engage:

Day 4

Hope

Lamentations 3:25-26

The LORD is good to those who wait for him, to the soul who seeks him. 26 It is good that one should wait quietly for the salvation of the LORD.

Write it:

Reflect:

Engage:

Day 5

Ephesians 1:18

Having the eyes of your hearts enlightened, that you may know what is the hope to which he has called you, what are the riches of his glorious inheritance in the saints.

Write it:

Reflect:

Engage:

Just

Yahweh

Just

Ephesians 4:32

Be kind to one another, tenderhearted,
forgiving one another, as God in Christ forgave you.

Write it:

Reflect:

Engage:

Day 2

Just

Psalm 103:8-10

The LORD works righteousness and justice for all who are oppressed. ⁷ He made known his ways to Moses, his acts to the people of Israel. ⁸ The LORD is merciful and gracious, slow to anger and abounding in steadfast love. ⁹ He will not always chide, nor will he keep his anger forever. ¹⁰ He does not deal with us according to our sins, nor repay us according to our iniquities.

Write it:

Reflect:

Engage:

63

Day 3

Just

Isaiah 9:7

O f the increase of his government and of peace there will be no end, on the throne of David and over his kingdom, to establish it and to uphold it with justice and with righteousness from this time forth and forevermore. The zeal of the LORD of hosts will do this.

Write it:

Reflect:

Engage:

Day 4

Just

Romans 8:30-31

A nd those whom he predestined he also called, and those whom he called he also justified, and those whom he justified he also glorified. What then shall we say to these things? If God is for us, who can be[1] against us?

Write it:

Reflect:

Engage:

Day 5

Just

Psalm 146:5-7

Blessed is he whose help is the God of Jacob, whose hope is in the LORD his God, ⁶ who made heaven and earth, the sea, and all that is in them,
who keeps faith forever; ⁷ who executes justice for the oppressed, who gives food to the hungry.

Write it:

Reflect:

Engage:

Part 2

Rooted in Promises

W e will be taking a slow stroll through the Psalms as we devour the goodness and faithfulness of God and His promises.

The Psalms are a book of prayer. Not just a book to study. More of a book to absorb, read aloud, a feeding for your soul. When you need solace, celebration, reassurance or repentance. The Psalms give way for emotions to move from inside yourself to the exterior as they are spoken into your day.

Spending the last couple weeks meditating on "Who" God is, should have opened up truth and clarity of His divine character. Now we will progress into what His promises "ARE".

Promise – A declaration or assurance that one will do a particular thing, or that a particular thing will happen.

Thinking of the word promise may stir up feeling that you would much rather push down. You may have had many broken promises thrown your way. Maybe you were the promise breaker for a time or season.

Here is the thing… We are looking not inward, but outward, to a God who does what He says He will do, NEVER breaking that declaration. Period! This is not about us, but Him.

Below are some steps I take when meditating through the Psalms. Again… there is no time limit or day that you have to read. Take 2-3 days on one passage if you need to. Again, I purposefully use scripture as the center focus, not my words. The goal here is to be fully engaged in His Word. Open up your reading time with a prayer asking God to empty out what is not of him and asking Him to fill you with His wisdom is a great way to begin each reading.

> **Read:** Through the passage once silently, then once out loud.
> **Write:** Use the space provided to write out the passage completely.
> **Reflect:** What does this passage say about God and what He promises to you? Go back and circle words that you feel He is speaking to you.
> **Engage:** Spend quiet minutes just hearing His voice wash over you, speaking into your heart and mind. Go over your circled words and ask God to reveal His heart to you.

He Is

With Us

With Us

Psalm 46

God is our refuge and strength, a very present[b] help in trouble.
² Therefore we will not fear though the earth gives way,
   though the mountains be moved into the heart of the sea,
³ though its waters roar and foam,
   though the mountains tremble at its swelling. *Selah*
⁴ There is a river whose streams make glad the city of God,
   the holy habitation of the Most High.
⁵ God is in the midst of her; she shall not be moved;
   God will help her when morning dawns.
⁶ The nations rage, the kingdoms totter;
   he utters his voice, the earth melts.
⁷ The LORD of hosts is with us;
   the God of Jacob is our fortress. *Selah*
⁸ Come, behold the works of the LORD,
   how he has brought desolations on the earth.
⁹ He makes wars cease to the end of the earth;
   he breaks the bow and shatters the spear;
   he burns the chariots with fire.
¹⁰ "Be still, and know that I am God.
   I will be exalted among the nations,
   I will be exalted in the earth!"
¹¹ The LORD of hosts is with us;
   the God of Jacob is our fortress. *Selah*

Write it:

Reflect:

Engage:

He

Delivers

Deliver

Psalm 34

I will bless the LORD at all times;
  his praise shall continually be in my mouth.
2 My soul makes its boast in the LORD;
  let the humble hear and be glad.
3 Oh, magnify the LORD with me,
  and let us exalt his name together!
4 I sought the LORD, and he answered me
  and delivered me from all my fears.
5 Those who look to him are radiant,
  and their faces shall never be ashamed.
6 This poor man cried, and the LORD heard him
  and saved him out of all his troubles.
7 The angel of the LORD encamps
  around those who fear him, and delivers them.
8 Oh, taste and see that the LORD is good!
  Blessed is the man who takes refuge in him!
9 Oh, fear the LORD, you his saints,
  for those who fear him have no lack!
10 The young lions suffer want and hunger;
  but those who seek the LORD lack no good thing.
11 Come, O children, listen to me;
  I will teach you the fear of the LORD.
12 What man is there who desires life
  and loves many days, that he may see good?
13 Keep your tongue from evil
  and your lips from speaking deceit.

¹⁴ Turn away from evil and do good;
    seek peace and pursue it.
¹⁵ The eyes of the LORD are toward the righteous
    and his ears toward their cry.
¹⁶ The face of the LORD is against those who do evil,
    to cut off the memory of them from the earth.
¹⁷ When the righteous cry for help, the LORD hears
    and delivers them out of all their troubles.
¹⁸ The LORD is near to the brokenhearted
    and saves the crushed in spirit.
¹⁹ Many are the afflictions of the righteous,
    but the LORD delivers him out of them all.
²⁰ He keeps all his bones;
    not one of them is broken.
²¹ Affliction will slay the wicked,
    and those who hate the righteous will be condemned.
²² The LORD redeems the life of his servants;
    none of those who take refuge in him will be condemned.

Write it:

Reflect:

Engage:

77

He

Restores

Restores

Psalm 51

Have mercy on me,[a] O God, according to your steadfast love;
according to your abundant mercy blot out my
transgressions.
2 Wash me thoroughly from my iniquity,
and cleanse me from my sin!
3 For I know my transgressions,
and my sin is ever before me.
4 Against you, you only, have I sinned
and done what is evil in your sight,
so that you may be justified in your words
and blameless in your judgment.
5 Behold, I was brought forth in iniquity,
and in sin did my mother conceive me.
6 Behold, you delight in truth in the inward being,
and you teach me wisdom in the secret heart.
7 Purge me with hyssop, and I shall be clean;
wash me, and I shall be whiter than snow.
8 Let me hear joy and gladness;
let the bones that you have broken rejoice.
9 Hide your face from my sins,
and blot out all my iniquities.
10 Create in me a clean heart, O God,
and renew a right[b] spirit within me.
11 Cast me not away from your presence,
and take not your Holy Spirit from me.

¹² Restore to me the joy of your salvation,
and uphold me with a willing spirit.
¹³ Then I will teach transgressors your ways,
and sinners will return to you.
¹⁴ Deliver me from bloodguiltiness, O God,
O God of my salvation,
and my tongue will sing aloud of your righteousness.
¹⁵ O Lord, open my lips,
and my mouth will declare your praise.
¹⁶ For you will not delight in sacrifice, or I would give it;
you will not be pleased with a burnt offering.
¹⁷ The sacrifices of God are a broken spirit;
a broken and contrite heart, O God, you will not despise.
¹⁸ Do good to Zion in your good pleasure;
build up the walls of Jerusalem;
¹⁹ then will you delight in right sacrifices,
in burnt offerings and whole burnt offerings;
then bulls will be offered on your altar.

Write it:

Reflect:

Engage:

81

He Is

Our Strength

Our Strength

Psalm 18

I love you, O LORD, my strength.
²The LORD is my rock and my fortress and my deliverer, my God,
my rock, in whom I take refuge,
  my shield, and the horn of my salvation, my stronghold.
³I call upon the LORD, who is worthy to be praised,
  and I am saved from my enemies.
⁴The cords of death encompassed me;
  the torrents of destruction assailed me;[a]
⁵the cords of Sheol entangled me;
  the snares of death confronted me.
⁶In my distress I called upon the LORD;
  to my God I cried for help.
From his temple he heard my voice,
  and my cry to him reached his ears.
⁷Then the earth reeled and rocked;
  the foundations also of the mountains trembled
  and quaked, because he was angry.
⁸Smoke went up from his nostrils,[b]
  and devouring fire from his mouth;
  glowing coals flamed forth from him.
⁹He bowed the heavens and came down;
  thick darkness was under his feet.
¹⁰He rode on a cherub and flew;
  he came swiftly on the wings of the wind.
¹¹He made darkness his covering, his canopy around him,
  thick clouds dark with water.

¹² Out of the brightness before him
hailstones and coals of fire broke through his clouds.
¹³ The LORD also thundered in the heavens,
and the Most High uttered his voice,
hailstones and coals of fire.
¹⁴ And he sent out his arrows and scattered them;
he flashed forth lightning's and routed them.
¹⁵ Then the channels of the sea were seen,
and the foundations of the world were laid bare
at your rebuke, O LORD,
at the blast of the breath of your nostrils.
¹⁶ He sent from on high, he took me;
he drew me out of many waters.
¹⁷ He rescued me from my strong enemy
and from those who hated me,
for they were too mighty for me.
¹⁸ They confronted me in the day of my calamity,
but the LORD was my support.
¹⁹ He brought me out into a broad place;
he rescued me, because he delighted in me.
²⁰ The LORD dealt with me according to my righteousness;
according to the cleanness of my hands he rewarded me.
²¹ For I have kept the ways of the LORD,
and have not wickedly departed from my God.
²² For all his rules[c] were before me,
and his statutes I did not put away from me.
²³ I was blameless before him,
and I kept myself from my guilt.
²⁴ So the LORD has rewarded me according to my righteousness,
according to the cleanness of my hands in his sight.
²⁵ With the merciful you show yourself merciful;
with the blameless man you show yourself blameless;
²⁶ with the purified you show yourself pure;
and with the crooked you make yourself seem tortuous.
²⁷ For you save a humble people,
but the haughty eyes you bring down.
²⁸ For it is you who light my lamp;
the LORD my God lightens my darkness.
²⁹ For by you I can run against a troop,

and by my God I can leap over a wall.
30 This God—his way is perfect;[d]
   the word of the LORD proves true;
   he is a shield for all those who take refuge in him.
31 For who is God, but the LORD?
   And who is a rock, except our God?—
32 the God who equipped me with strength
   and made my way blameless.
33 He made my feet like the feet of a deer
   and set me secure on the heights.
34 He trains my hands for war,
   so that my arms can bend a bow of bronze.
35 You have given me the shield of your salvation,
   and your right hand supported me,
   and your gentleness made me great.
36 You gave a wide place for my steps under me,
   and my feet did not slip.
37 I pursued my enemies and overtook them,
   and did not turn back till they were consumed.
38 I thrust them through, so that they were not able to rise;
   they fell under my feet.
39 For you equipped me with strength for the battle;
   you made those who rise against me sink under me.
40 You made my enemies turn their backs to me,[e]
   and those who hated me I destroyed.
41 They cried for help, but there was none to save;
   they cried to the LORD, but he did not answer them.
42 I beat them fine as dust before the wind;
   I cast them out like the mire of the streets.
43 You delivered me from strife with the people;
   you made me the head of the nations;
   people whom I had not known served me.
44 As soon as they heard of me they obeyed me;
   foreigners came cringing to me.
45 Foreigners lost heart
   and came trembling out of their fortresses.
46 The LORD lives, and blessed be my rock,
   and exalted be the God of my salvation—

⁴⁷ the God who gave me vengeance
    and subdued peoples under me,
⁴⁸ who rescued me from my enemies;
    yes, you exalted me above those who rose against me;
    you delivered me from the man of violence.
⁴⁹ For this I will praise you, O LORD, among the nations,
    and sing to your name.
⁵⁰ Great salvation he brings to his king,
    and shows steadfast love to his anointed,
    to David and his offspring forever.

Write it:

Reflect:

Engage:

89

He Is

Trustworthy

Trustworthy

Psalm 20

May the LORD answer you in the day of trouble! May the name of the God of Jacob protect you! ² May he send you help from the sanctuary and give you support from Zion! ³ May he remember all your offerings and regard with favor your burnt sacrifices! *Selah*

⁴ May he grant you your heart's desire and fulfill all your plans! ⁵ May we shout for joy over your salvation, and in the name of our God set up our banners! May the LORD fulfill all your petitions! ⁶ Now I know that the LORD saves his anointed; he will answer him from his holy heaven with the saving might of his right hand. ⁷ Some trust in chariots and some in horses, but we trust in the name of the LORD our God. ⁸ They collapse and fall but we rise and stand upright. ⁹ O LORD, save the king! May he answer us when we call.

Write it:

Reflect:

Engage:

He Is

Hope

Psalm 27

The LORD is my light and my salvation; whom shall I fear?

The LORD is the stronghold[a] of my life; of whom shall I be afraid?
2 When evildoers assail me
   to eat up my flesh,
my adversaries and foes,
   it is they who stumble and fall.
3 Though an army encamp against me,
   my heart shall not fear;
though war arise against me,
   yet[b] I will be confident.
4 One thing have I asked of the LORD,
   that will I seek after:
that I may dwell in the house of the LORD
   all the days of my life,
to gaze upon the beauty of the LORD
   and to inquire[c] in his temple.
5 For he will hide me in his shelter
   in the day of trouble;
he will conceal me under the cover of his tent;
   he will lift me high upon a rock.
6 And now my head shall be lifted up
   above my enemies all around me,
and I will offer in his tent

sacrifices with shouts of joy;
I will sing and make melody to the LORD.
7 Hear, O LORD, when I cry aloud;
    be gracious to me and answer me!
8 You have said, "Seek[d] my face."
My heart says to you,
    "Your face, LORD, do I seek."[c]
9   Hide not your face from me.
Turn not your servant away in anger,
    O you who have been my help.
Cast me not off; forsake me not,
    O God of my salvation!
10 For my father and my mother have forsaken me,
    but the LORD will take me in.
11 Teach me your way, O LORD,
    and lead me on a level path
    because of my enemies.
12 Give me not up to the will of my adversaries;
    for false witnesses have risen against me,
    and they breathe out violence.
13 I believe that I shall look[f] upon the goodness of the LORD
    in the land of the living!
14 Wait for the LORD;
    be strong, and let your heart take courage;
    wait for the LORD!

Write it:

Reflect:

Engage:

97

He Is

Merciful

Psalm 32

Blessed is the one whose transgression is forgiven, whose sin is covered.

² Blessed is the man against whom the LORD counts no iniquity,
    and in whose spirit there is no deceit.
³ For when I kept silent, my bones wasted away
    through my groaning all day long.
⁴ For day and night your hand was heavy upon me;
    my strength was dried up as by the heat of summer. *Selah*
⁵ I acknowledged my sin to you,
    and I did not cover my iniquity;
I said, "I will confess my transgressions to the LORD,"
    and you forgave the iniquity of my sin. *Selah*
⁶ Therefore let everyone who is godly
    offer prayer to you at a time when you may be found;
surely in the rush of great waters,
    they shall not reach him.
⁷ You are a hiding place for me;
    you preserve me from trouble;
    you surround me with shouts of deliverance. *Selah*
⁸ I will instruct you and teach you in the way you should go;
    I will counsel you with my eye upon you.
⁹ Be not like a horse or a mule, without understanding,
    which must be curbed with bit and bridle,
    or it will not stay near you.

[10] Many are the sorrows of the wicked,
  but steadfast love surrounds the one who trusts in the LORD.
[11] Be glad in the LORD, and rejoice, O righteous,
  and shout for joy, all you upright in heart!

Write it:

Reflect:

Engage:

101

He

Redeems

Redeems

Psalm 40

I waited patiently for the LORD;

he inclined to me and heard my cry.
² He drew me up from the pit of destruction,
  out of the miry bog,
and set my feet upon a rock,
  making my steps secure.
³ He put a new song in my mouth,
  a song of praise to our God.
Many will see and fear,
  and put their trust in the LORD.
⁴ Blessed is the man who makes
  the LORD his trust,
who does not turn to the proud,
  to those who go astray after a lie!
⁵ You have multiplied, O LORD my God,
  your wondrous deeds and your thoughts toward us;
  none can compare with you!
I will proclaim and tell of them,
  yet they are more than can be told.
⁶ In sacrifice and offering you have not delighted,
  but you have given me an open ear.
Burnt offering and sin offering

you have not required.
⁷ Then I said, "Behold, I have come;
   in the scroll of the book it is written of me:
⁸ I delight to do your will, O my God;
   your law is within my heart."
⁹ I have told the glad news of deliverance[o]
   in the great congregation;
behold, I have not restrained my lips,
   as you know, O LORD.
¹⁰ I have not hidden your deliverance within my heart;
   I have spoken of your faithfulness and your salvation;
I have not concealed your steadfast love and your faithfulness from
the great congregation.
¹¹ As for you, O LORD, you will not restrain your mercy from me;
your steadfast love and your faithfulness will
ever preserve me! ¹² For evils have encompassed me beyond number;
my iniquities have overtaken me,
and I cannot see; they are more than the hairs of my head; my
heart fails me.
¹³ Be pleased, O LORD, to deliver me!
   O LORD, make haste to help me!
¹⁴ Let those be put to shame and disappointed altogether
   who seek to snatch away my life;
let those be turned back and brought to dishonor
   who delight in my hurt!
¹⁵ Let those be appalled because of their shame
   who say to me, "Aha, Aha!"
¹⁶ But may all who seek you
   rejoice and be glad in you;
may those who love your salvation
   say continually, "Great is the LORD!"
¹⁷ As for me, I am poor and needy,
   but the Lord takes thought for me.
You are my help and my deliverer;
   do not delay, O my God!

Write it:

Reflect:

Engage:

He Is

Worthy

Psalm 145

I will extol you, my God and King, and bless your name forever and

ever.
2 Every day I will bless you
   and praise your name forever and ever.
3 Great is the LORD, and greatly to be praised,
   and his greatness is unsearchable. 4 One generation shall commend your
works to another, and shall declare your mighty acts. 5 On the glorious
splendor of your majesty,
   and on your wondrous works, I will meditate.
6 They shall speak of the might of your awesome deeds,
   and I will declare your greatness.
7 They shall pour forth the fame of your abundant goodness
   and shall sing aloud of your righteousness.

8 The LORD is gracious and merciful,
   slow to anger and abounding in steadfast love.
9 The LORD is good to all,
   and his mercy is over all that he has made.
10 All your works shall give thanks to you, O LORD,
   and all your saints shall bless you!
11 They shall speak of the glory of your kingdom
   and tell of your power,
12 to make known to the children of man your[b] mighty deeds, and the

glorious splendor of your kingdom.
¹³ Your kingdom is an everlasting kingdom,
and your dominion endures throughout all generations.
[The LORD is faithful in all his words
    and kind in all his works.][c]
¹⁴ The LORD upholds all who are falling
    and raises up all who are bowed down.
¹⁵ The eyes of all look to you,
    and you give them their food in due season.
¹⁶ You open your hand;
    you satisfy the desire of every living thing.
¹⁷ The LORD is righteous in all his ways
    and kind in all his works.
¹⁸ The LORD is near to all who call on him,
    to all who call on him in truth.
¹⁹ He fulfills the desire of those who fear him;
    he also hears their cry and saves them.
²⁰ The LORD preserves all who love him,
    but all the wicked he will destroy.
²¹ My mouth will speak the praise of the LORD,
    and let all flesh bless his holy name forever and ever.

Write it:

Reflect:

Engage:

109

Part 3

Rooted in Truth

Christ himself is filled with grace and truth.

Let's tilt the scale towards grace, beauty, excellence and mercy. Because Christ, his life and the truth that lives there, is all that matters. When we take the focus off of self, we are the most authentic self, we can be. In Romans 7 Paul goes on for quite a bit in frustration on what he wants to do, yet does something else. Then in verse 25 he finds the answer "Thanks be to God *through* Jesus Christ our Lord."

This reminder tears our attention away from our self-loathing, self-sacrificing, shamed filled thoughts. Reminding us to get back to the businesses of who we are meant to be, who we already are in Christ! What freedom that should bring our weary souls. God does not need us, He wants us.

Accepting the fact that we are beloved by God... That's it. This will start to pull at the weeds of self-doubt. It will enable us to lose ourselves in surrender, replacing insecurity with the insurmountable truth that we are His beloved. He wants dominion over every portion of our hearts.

Believing that we are precious to the King of Creation, not just a waste of space, starts with the true belief that we are not irrelevant.

The Word speaks much about how God sees, feels and desires to interact with us. We are walking temples of the Holy Spirit. God is making us a kingdom, washing us with love that we have the ability to sprinkle into others through the way we live.

No sprinkling can happen though, until we claim the truths he has spoken over us. If we want to walk the path of His humble, mercy filled servant. We are wise to set fire to our rights, expectations, and worries. We first have to believe, then proclaim the truths he has given us into the fabric of our souls.

Let's dive into 10 truths God speaks over us. You Are... Whole, Known, Loved, Enough, Protected, Forgiven, Redeemed, Pure, Free & Welcomed.

As we journey through these truths. Use these 4 methods to dive deeper into understanding each scripture reading.

> ***Read:*** Through the passage once silently, then once out loud.
> ***Write:*** Use the space provided to write out the passage.
> ***Reflect:*** Go back and circle words that you feel He is speaking to you, pertaining to the "You Are' topic.
> ***Engage:*** Spend quiet minutes just hearing His voice wash over you, speaking into your heart and mind. Go over your circled words and ask God to reveal His heart to you.

You Are

Whole

Day 1

Whole

Psalm 30:6-7

As for me, I said in my prosperity "I shall never be moved." By your favor, O LORD, you made my mountains stand strong; you hid your face; I was dismayed.

Write it:

Reflect:

Engage:

Day 2

Whole

Psalm 18:2

The LORD is my rock and my fortress and my deliverer, my God, my rock, in whom I take refuge, my shield, and the horn of my salvation, my stronghold.

Write it:

Reflect:

Engage:

Day 3

Whole

Psalm 63:1-2

O God, you are my God; earnestly I seek you; my soul thirsts for you; my flesh faints for you, as in a dry and weary land where there is no water.
So I have looked upon you in the sanctuary, beholding your power and glory.

Write it:

Reflect:

Engage:

Day 4

Psalm 63:3-4

Because your steadfast love is better than life, my lips will praise you. So I will bless you as long as I live; in your name I will lift up my hands.

Write it:

Reflect:

Engage:

Day 5

Whole

Psalm 103:2-5

O Bless the LORD, O my soul, and forget not all his benefits, [3] who forgives all your iniquity,
who heals all your diseases, [4] who redeems your life from the pit, who crowns you with steadfast love and mercy, [5] who satisfies you with good so that your youth is renewed like the eagles.

Write it:

Reflect:

Engage:

117

You Are

Known

Day 1

Known

Psalm 139:1-3

O LORD, you have searched me and known me! [2] You know when I sit down and when I rise up; You discern my thoughts from afar. [3] You search out my path and my lying down and are acquainted with all my ways.

Write it:

Reflect:

Engage:

Day 2

Known

Psalm 139:4-6

E ven before a word is on my tongue, behold, O LORD, you know it altogether. ⁵ You hem me in, behind and before, and lay your hand upon me. ⁶ Such knowledge is too wonderful for me; it is high; I cannot attain it.

Write it:

Reflect:

Engage:

Day 3

Known

Psalm 139: 7-10

Where shall I go from your Spirit? Or where shall I flee from your presence? [8] If I ascend to heaven, you are there! If I make my bed in Sheol, you are there! [9] If I take the wings of the morning and dwell in the uttermost parts of the sea, [10] even there your hand shall lead me, and your right hand shall hold me.

Write it:

Reflect:

Engage:

Day 4

Known

Psalm 139:13-14

For you formed my inward parts; you knitted me together in my mother's womb. [14] I praise you, for I am fearfully and wonderfully made. Wonderful are your works; my soul knows it very well.

Write it:

Reflect:

Engage:

Day 5

Known

Psalm 139:23-24

Search me, O God, and know my heart! Try me and know my thoughts![s] 24 And see if there be any grievous way in me, and lead me in the way everlasting!

Write it:

Reflect:

Engage:

You Are

Loved

Day 1

Loved

Psalm 89:1-2

I will sing of the steadfast love of the LORD, forever;
with my mouth I will make known your faithfulness to all
generations. ² For I said, "Steadfast love will be built up forever; in the
heavens you will establish your faithfulness."

Write it:

Reflect:

Engage

Day 2

Loved

Psalm 89:3-4

You have said, "I have made a covenant with my chosen one; I have sworn to David my servant: 4 'I will establish your offspring forever, and build your throne for all generations. *Selah*

Write it:

Reflect:

Engage:

Day 3

Loved

Psalm 89:24-27

My faithfulness and my steadfast love shall be with him, and in my name shall his horn be exalted. 25 I will set his hand on the sea and his right hand on the rivers. 26 He shall cry to me, 'You are my Father, my God, and the Rock of my salvation.' 27 And I will make him the firstborn, the highest of the kings of the earth.

Write it:

Reflect:

Engage:

127

Day 4

Loved

Psalm 89:28-29

My steadfast love I will keep for him forever, and my covenant will stand firm[d] for him. [29] I will establish his offspring forever and his throne as the days of the heavens.

Write it:

Reflect:

Engage:

Day 5

Loved

Psalm 69:16-18

Answer me, O LORD, for your steadfast love is good; according to your abundant mercy, turn to me. [17] Hide not your face from your servant, for I am in distress; make haste to answer me. [18] Draw near to my soul, redeem me; ransom me because of my enemies!

Write it:

Reflect:

Engage:

You Are

Enough

Day 1

Enough

Psalm 42:8

B y day the LORD commands his steadfast love, and at night his song is with me, a prayer to the God of my life.

Write it:

Reflect:

Engage:

131

Enough

Psalm 16:5-6

The LORD is my chosen portion and my cup; you hold my lot. ⁶ The lines have fallen for me in pleasant places; indeed, I have a beautiful inheritance.

Write it:

Reflect:

Engage:

Day 3

Enough

Psalm 16:7-8

I bless the LORD who gives me counsel; in the night also my heart instructs me.[u] 8 I have set the LORD always before me; because he is at my right hand, I shall not be shaken.

Write it:

Reflect:

Engage:

Day 4

Enough

Psalm 16:11

ou make known to me the path of life; in your presence there is fullness of joy; at your right hand are pleasures forevermore.

Write it:

Reflect:

Engage:

Day 5

Enough

2 Corinthians 2:15

or we are the aroma of Christ to God among those who are being saved and among those who are perishing,

Write it:

Reflect:

Engage:

You Are

Protected

Day 1

Protected

Psalm 9:7-10

But the LORD sits enthroned forever; he has established his throne for justice, 8 and he judges the world with righteousness; he judges the peoples with uprightness. 9 The LORD is a stronghold for the oppressed, a stronghold in times of trouble. 10 And those who know your name put their trust in you, for you, O LORD, have not forsaken those who seek you.

Write it:

Reflect:

Engage:

Day 2

Protected

Psalm 89:33-35

But I will not remove from him my steadfast love or be false to my faithfulness. [34] I will not violate my covenant or alter the word that went forth from my lips.
[35] Once for all I have sworn by my holiness; I will not lie to David.

Write it:

Reflect:

Engage:

Day 3

Protected

Psalm 63:5-8

My soul will be satisfied as with fat and rich food, and my mouth will praise you with joyful lips, ⁶ when I remember you upon my bed, and meditate on you in the watches of the night; ⁷ for you have been my help, and in the shadow of your wings I will sing for joy. ⁸ My soul clings to you; your right hand upholds me.

Write it:

Reflect:

Engage:

Day 4

Protected

Psalm 63:9-11

But those who seek to destroy my life shall go down into the depths of the earth; [10] they shall be given over to the power of the sword; they shall be a portion for jackals. [11] But the king shall rejoice in God; all who swear by him shall exult, for the mouths of liars will be stopped.

Write it:

Reflect:

Engage:

Day 5

Psalm 91:4

 e will cover you with his pinions, and under his wings you will find refuge; his faithfulness is a shield and buckler.

Write it:

Reflect:

Engage:

141

You Are

Forgiven

Day 1

Forgiven

Psalm 145:8-9

The LORD is gracious and merciful, slow to anger and abounding in steadfast love. The LORD is good to all, and his mercy is over all that he has made.

Write it:

Reflect:

Engage:

Day 2

Forgiven

Psalm 16:9-10

Therefore my heart is glad, and my whole being[c] rejoices; my flesh also dwells secure. [10] For you will not abandon my soul to Sheol, or let your holy one see corruption.

Write it:

Reflect:

Engage:

Day 3

Forgiven

Psalm 10:16-18

T he LORD is king forever and ever; the nations perish from his land. [17] O LORD, you hear the desire of the afflicted; you will strengthen their heart; you will incline your ear [18] to do justice to the fatherless and the oppressed, so that man who is of the earth may strike terror no more.

Write it:

Reflect:

Engage:

Day 4

Forgiven

Psalm 103:10-12

He does not deal with us according to our sins, nor repay us according to our iniquities. [11] For as high as the heavens are above the earth, so great is his steadfast love toward those who fear him; [12] as far as the east is from the west, so far does he remove our transgressions from us.

Write it:

Reflect:

Engage:

Day 5

Forgiven

Psalm 103:13-14

As a father shows compassion to his children, so the LORD shows compassion to those who fear him. [14] For he knows our frame;[a] he remembers that we are dust.

Write it:

Reflect:

Engage:

You Are

Redeemed

Day 1

Redeemed

Psalm 9:18-20

For the needy shall not always be forgotten, and the hope of the poor shall not perish forever. [19] Arise, O LORD! Let not man prevail; let the nations be judged before you! [20] Put them in fear, O LORD! Let the nations know that they are but men! *Selah*

Write it:

Reflect:

Engage:

Day 2

Redeemed

Psalm 145:14-15

The LORD upholds all who are falling and raises up all who are bowed down. ¹⁵ The eyes of all look to you, and you give them their food in due season.

Write it:

Reflect:

Engage:

Day 3

Redeemed

Psalm 145:17-20

The LORD is righteous in all his ways and kind in all his works. [18] The LORD is near to all who call on him, to all who call on him in truth. [19] He fulfills the desire of those who fear him: he also hears their cry and saves them. [20] The LORD preserves all who love him, but all the wicked he will destroy.

Write it:

Reflect:

Engage:

151

Day 4

Redeemed

Psalm 62:1-2

For God alone my soul waits in silence; from him comes my salvation. ² He alone is my rock and my salvation, my fortress; I shall not be greatly shaken.

Write it:

Reflect:

Engage:

Day 5

Redeemed

Psalm 62:5-7

For God alone, O my soul, wait in silence, for my hope is from him. ⁶ He only is my rock and my salvation, my fortress; I shall not be shaken. ⁷ On God rests my salvation and my glory; my mighty rock, my refuge is God.

Write it:

Reflect:

Engage:

You Are

Pure

Day 1

Pure

Psalm 57:9-10

I will give thanks to you, O Lord, among the peoples; I will sing praises to you among the nations. [10] For your steadfast love is great to the heavens, your faithfulness to the clouds.

Write it:

Reflect:

Engage:

Day 2

Pure

Psalm 1:1-2

Blessed is the man[a] who walks not in the counsel of the wicked, nor stands in the way of sinners, nor sits in the seat of scoffers; 2 but his delight is in the law[b] of the LORD, and on his law he meditates day and night.

Write it:

Reflect:

Engage:

Day 3

Pure

Psalm 1:3-4

He is like a tree planted by streams of water that yields its fruit in its season, and its leaf does not wither. In all that he does, he prospers. ⁴ The wicked are not so, but are like chaff that the wind drives away.

Write it:

Reflect:

Engage:

Day 4

Pure

Psalm 51:10

C reate in me a clean heart, O God, and renew a right[b] spirit within me.

Write it:

Reflect:

Engage:

Day 5

Pure

Psalm 24:3-4

W ho shall ascend the hill of the LORD? And who shall stand in his holy place? [4] He who has clean hands and a pure heart, who does not lift up his soul to what is false and does not swear deceitfully.

Write it:

Reflect:

Engage:

You Are

Free

Day 1

Psalm 9:1-2

I will give thanks to the LORD with my whole heart; I will recount all of your wonderful deeds. ² I will be glad and exult in you; I will sing praise to your name, O Most High.

Write it:

Reflect:

Engage:

Day 2

Free

Psalm 30:1-3

I will extol you, O LORD, for you have drawn me up and have not let my foes rejoice over me. ² O LORD my God, I cried to you for help, and you have healed me. ³ O LORD, you have brought up my soul from Sheol; you restored me to life from among those who go down to the pit.

Write it:

Reflect:

Engage:

Day 3

Free

Psalm 30:4-5

Sing praises to the LORD, O you his saints, and give thanks to his holy name. [5] For his anger is but for a moment, and his favor is for a lifetime. Weeping may tarry for the night, but joy comes with the morning.

Write it:

Reflect:

Engage:

Free

Psalm 30:11-12

You have turned for me my mourning into dancing; you have loosed my sackcloth and clothed me with gladness, [12] that my glory may sing your praise and not be silent. O LORD my God, I will give thanks to you forever!

Write it:

Reflect:

Engage:

Day 5

Free

Psalm 59:9-10

O my Strength, I will watch for you, for you, O God, are my fortress. [10] My God in his steadfast love[s] will meet me; God will let me look in triumph on my enemies.

Write it:

Reflect:

Engage:

You Are

Welcomed

Day 1

Welcomed

Psalm 2:7-8

I will tell of the decree: The LORD said to me, "You are my Son; today I have begotten you. [8] Ask of me, and I will make the nations your heritage, and the ends of the earth your possession.

Write it:

Reflect:

Engage:

167

Day 2

Welcomed

Psalm 75:9-10

B ut I will declare it forever; I will sing praises to the God of Jacob. ¹⁰ All the horns of the wicked I will cut off, but the horns of the righteous shall be lifted up.

Write it:

Reflect:

Engage:

Day 3

Welcomed

Psalm 13:5-6

B ut I have trusted in your steadfast love; my heart shall rejoice in your salvation. ⁶ I will sing to the LORD, because he has dealt bountifully with me.

Write it:

Reflect:

Engage:

Day 4

Welcomed

Psalm 86:5

For you, O Lord, are good and forgiving, abounding in steadfast love to all who call upon you.

Write it:

Reflect:

Engage:

Day 5

Welcomed

Psalm 125:1-2

Those who trust in the LORD are like Mount Zion, which cannot be moved, but abides forever. ² As the mountains surround Jerusalem, so the LORD surrounds his people, from this time forth and forevermore.

Write it:

Reflect:

Engage:

Closing

hat a journey! I pray you have been encouraged, challenged and strengthened through your time meditating in the Word. As you have gained tools, insight and patterns of absorbing His *Character, Promises & Truth*. I am hopeful that you will use what worked well for you. Perhaps creating some new habits on your devotional journey, that will become what you thirst for daily.

His Word has the power to do what we thought could never be and break open unimaginable barriers within our hearts. I so wish I could hear your story of seeking Him. I find peace in the truth that one day we will meet. We will be perfect and complete, lacking nothing that holds us captive here on earth. Oh, how wonderful that day will be. I will know you, and you me. All credited to His Word and the oneness it produces within us.

Until then my friend. My prayer for you is to live with intense purpose. *Rooted in the Word*, strengthened by truth, living an abundant life that oozes from each letter and promise it speaks. As we each cling to this abundant truth, running the race well. Let us live it purposefully until the last step!

Kele

About the Author

Kele is a coffee shop seeker, justice bearer, baby squeezer, tea drinker, missions director, disciple and all around goofy mom of 2 grown children & one in heaven. She lives her life with unashamed authenticity, which has been known to cause embarrassing moments for all involved! Her deep love for her God and people is the Joy of her life.

Kele is the founder of *Do Good Ministries*, a non-profit that serves at-risk youth globally. She is the author of *Purposefully Woven – Turning Tragedy & Trials to Triumph*. Currently residing in Texas.

Her life mantra of "Break my heart for what breaks yours Lord." has been a wild journey. A path of continual refining & redeeming.

You can order her books on Amazon and find out more about how to support her ministry work at: dogoodministries.com.